W9-CLV-075

Women in Space

Major Women in Science

Women in Anthropology

Women in Chemistry

Women in Engineering

Women in Information Technology

Women in Medicine

Women in Physics

Women in Space

Women in the Environmental Sciences

Women Inventors

Women Who Built
Our Scientific Foundations

MAJOR WOMEN IN SCIENCE

Women in Space

Shaina Indovino

Mason Crest

Mason Crest
450 Parkway Drive, Suite D
Broomall, Pennsylvania 19008
www.masoncrest.com

Printed and bound in the United States of America.

First printing
9 8 7 6 5 4 3 2 1

Series ISBN: 978-1-4222-2923-1
ISBN: 978-1-4222-2931-6
ebook ISBN: 978-1-4222-8900-6

The Library of Congress has cataloged the
hardcopy format(s) as follows:

Library of Congress Cataloging-in-Publication Data

Indovino, Shaina Carmel.
Women in space / Shaina Indovino.
p. cm. -- (Major women in science)
Audience: 12.
Audience: Grades 7 to 8.
Includes index.
ISBN 978-1-4222-2931-6 (hardcover) -- ISBN 978-1-4222-2923-1 (series) -- ISBN 978-1-4222-8900-6 (ebook)
1. Women astronauts--Juvenile literature. 2. Women astronauts--Biography--Juvenile literature. 3. Astronautics--History--Juvenile literature. 4. Astronautics--Biography--Juvenile literature. I. Title.
TL789.85.A1I53 2014
629.45'0092'2--dc23
2013009826

Produced by Vestal Creative Services.
www.vestalcreative.com

Contents

Introduction

Have you wondered about how the natural world works? Are you curious about how science could help sick people get better? Do you want to learn more about our planet and universe? Are you excited to use technology to learn and share ideas? Do you want to build something new?

Scientists, engineers, and doctors are among the many types of people who think deeply about science and nature, who often have new ideas on how to improve life in our world.

We live in a remarkable time in human history. The level of understanding and rate of progress in science and technology have never been greater. Major advances in these areas include the following:

- Computer scientists and engineers are building mobile and Internet technology to help people access and share information at incredible speeds.
- Biologists and chemists are creating medicines that can target and get rid of harmful cancer cells in the body.
- Engineers are guiding robots on Mars to explore the history of water on that planet.
- Physicists are using math and experiments to estimate the age of the universe to be greater than 13 billion years old.
- Scientists and engineers are building hybrid cars that can be better for our environment.

Scientists are interested in discovering and understanding key principles in nature, including biological, chemical, mathematical, and physical aspects of our world. Scientists observe, measure, and experiment in a systematic way in order to test and improve their understanding. Engineers focus on applying scientific knowledge and math to find creative solutions for technical problems and to develop real products for people to use. There are many types of engineering, including computer, electrical, mechanical, civil, chemical, and biomedical engineering. Some people have also found that studying science or engineering can help them succeed in other professions such as law, business, and medicine.

Both women and men can be successful in science and engineering. This book series highlights women leaders who have made significant contributions across many scientific fields, including chemistry, medicine, anthropology, engineering, and physics. Historically, women have faced barriers to training and building careers in science,

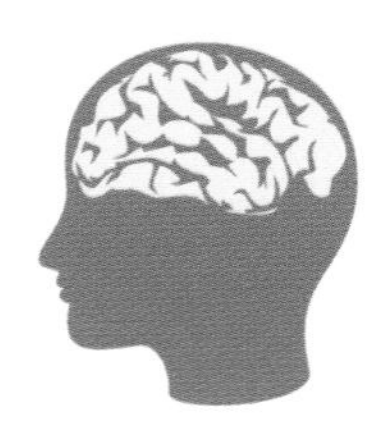

which makes some of these stories even more amazing. While not all barriers have been overcome, our society has made tremendous progress in educating and advancing women in science. Today, there are schools, organizations, and resources to enable women to pursue careers as scientists or engineers at the highest levels of achievement and leadership.

The goals of this series are to help you:

1. Learn about women scientists, engineers, doctors, and inventors who have made a major impact in science and our society
2. Understand different types of science and engineering
3. Explore science and math in school and real life

You can do a lot of things to learn more about science, math, and engineering. Explore topics in books or online, take a class at school, go to science camp, or do experiments at home. More important, talk to a real scientist! Call or e-mail your local college to find students and professors. They would love to meet with you. Ask your doctors about their education and training. Or you can check out these helpful resources:

- *Nova* has very cool videos about science, including profiles on real-life women scientists and engineers: www.pbs.org/wgbh/nova.
- *National Geographic* has excellent photos and stories to inspire people to care about the planet: science.nationalgeographic.com/science.
- Here are examples of online courses for students, of which many are free to use:
  1. Massachusetts Institute of Technology (MIT) OpenCourseWare highlights for high school: http://ocw.mit.edu/high-school
  2. Khan Academy tutorials and courses: www.khanacademy.org.
  3. Stanford University Online, featuring video courses and programs for middle and high school students: online.stanford.edu.

Other skills will become important as you get older. Build strong communication skills, such as asking questions and sharing your ideas in class. Ask for advice or help when needed from your teachers, mentors, tutors, or classmates. Be curious and resilient: learn from your successes and mistakes. The best scientists do.

Learning science and math is one of the most important things that you can do in school. Knowledge and experience in these areas will teach you how to think and how the world works and can provide you with many adventures and paths in life. I hope you will explore science—you could make a difference in this world.

Ann Lee-Karlon, PhD
President
Association for Women in Science
San Francisco, California

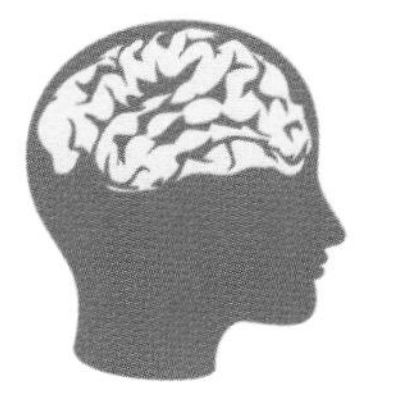

United States
USA

1

What Does It Take to Be an Astronaut?

Going into outer space is exciting—but getting there takes hard work. While many kids dream of one day becoming an astronaut, relatively few people are selected to go into space. In the United States, the National Aeronautics and Space Administration (NASA) controls all space missions. Other countries have different space organizations.

Before you can become an astronaut, you will need a lot of training. Then you must apply to be an astronaut. Astronauts must be well educated, very healthy,

Learning to fly an airplane could be a first step toward becoming an astronaut.

and knowledgeable in many areas. This is because an astronaut must fill many roles during a mission. An astronaut may need to steer the spaceship, repair technical problems, conduct experiments, or record data. Because an astronaut is far away from the Earth, he or she will need to be prepared for all sorts of situations. Anything can happen when you are out in space!

Even if you are qualified to be an astronaut, you are still competing with thousands of people. Only about 330 people in the United States have ever been chosen to train to become an astronaut. Becoming an astronaut is an opportunity of a lifetime.

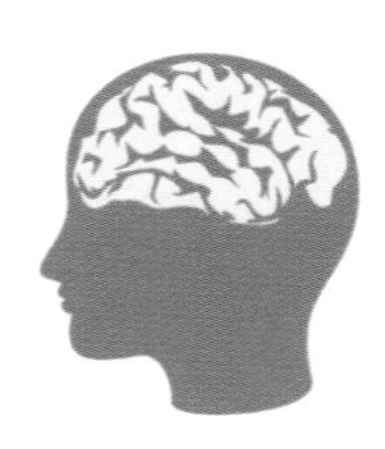

Many astronauts are former airplane pilots and **engineers**. Women were never common in either of these two fields. This might explain why the first group of astronauts was made up entirely of men. Today, this trend is changing. Plenty of women have become astronauts and many more are being selected.

Why Be an Astronaut?

Astronauts have some of the most exciting careers in the world. While most scientists are restricted to the ground, astronauts go out into space. Some of the discoveries made there are unlike anything we have ever known. Astronauts go into space with very specific assignments that allow us to plan new **missions** to conduct even more experiments.

Space science has been something humanity has been interested in for thousands of years. Ancient astronomers came up with many theories about what was beyond the Earth and in the sky. It wasn't until just a few hundred years ago that we realized our planet revolved around the Sun! Today, our knowledge about the universe is constantly expanding. We have traveled to the moon and sent probes to other planets. Humans are slowly discovering more about both space and **physics**. All of this would not have been possible without astronauts.

Education

Astronauts must be extremely well educated. This is because only a handful of applicants are selected. If you seriously want to become an astronaut, it is never too early to start! Begin researching space science and the history behind it. Consider studying engineering, math, and other sciences. When you are ready to go away to college, pick a major that you know will be useful in space. The minimum degree to become an astronaut is a bachelor's degree, but higher degrees are preferred. Today, there are a few majors intended for future astronauts, but the crew for a space mission must be **diverse**. As long as your area of study could be useful, you will be in the running.

You may put yourself at an advantage by studying more than one useful science. A woman who knows how to fly a plane and be an engineer is more likely to be chosen than a woman who only has knowledge in one area. Many women

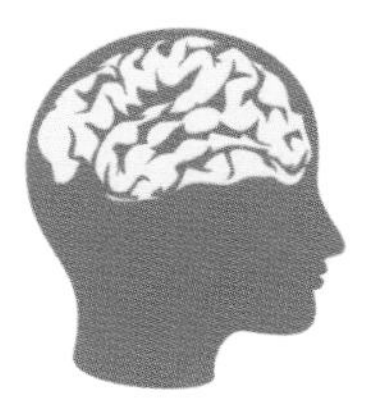

pursuing a career in space science also work for NASA before becoming an astronaut. This way, NASA knows the work they can do.

For the lucky few who have been chosen to be astronauts, it was worth the wait. They worked hard and reached for the stars—and they got there!

Character and Physical Condition

To be an astronaut, you must be willing to get used to a whole different way of life in space. How you move, eat, drink, and live will be unlike anything you have experienced before. Anyone who wants to be an astronaut must be prepared for this.

Being an astronaut takes some getting used to. Unlike on Earth, gravity is very weak in a space shuttle. Astronauts will float around if they don't hold onto something or strap themselves in. Being in space can also give you a special type of motion sickness. Astronauts must take the time to **adapt** to the change in gravity. Still, the feeling of weightlessness is not for everyone. As you can imagine, eating and drinking is very different without gravity. So is going to the bathroom!

After being selected as an astronaut, you must go through a lot of training. Big pools and wind tunnels are used to **simulate** low-gravity situations. Other machines are used to prepare you for the speed at which you'll travel into space. Future space pilots must practice how to fly a space shuttle by using simulators. An astronaut must be committed to being in shape so that he or she can handle the lack of exercise in space.

Space travel can be very lonely. Astronauts will spend weeks or even months with the same crew. Communication with the Earth is possible but limited. Astronauts miss their loved ones while they're away on a mission, and their families and friends miss them. An astronaut must be able to endure this situation.

An astronaut's daily needs are different from ours here on Earth. If astronauts spend weeks or months in space, what do they eat or drink? They can't cook food on the space ship, and they can't store enough water to survive for very long. NASA has found ways to **improvise**. Many astronauts eat prepackaged meals

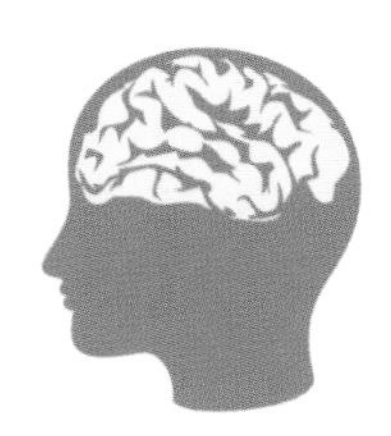

that don't need to be cooked. For water, astronauts rely on recycled fluids. These fluids come from the crew's breath and urine. Using a special **filtration** system, urine can be turned into water that is safe enough to drink!

So—do you think you have what it takes?

Words to Know

Engineers: people who design, build, and study machines, buildings, and other structures.

Missions: voyages outside of the earth's atmosphere, usually with the purpose of conducting scientific research.

Physics: the study of matter and energy, and the interaction between the two.

Diverse: having variety; distinctly different or unlike.

Adapt: to become used to.

Simulate: to pretend or imitate a situation.

Improvise: to manage with whatever materials are on hand.

Filtration: the process by which a substance is passed through a screen or other substance to get rid of unwanted parts.

Find Out More

How Stuff Works, "How Do I Become an Astronaut?"
science.howstuffworks.com/question534.htm

NASA
www.nasa.gov

Pogue, William R. *How Do You Go to the Bathroom in Space?* New York: Tom Doherty Associates, 2009.

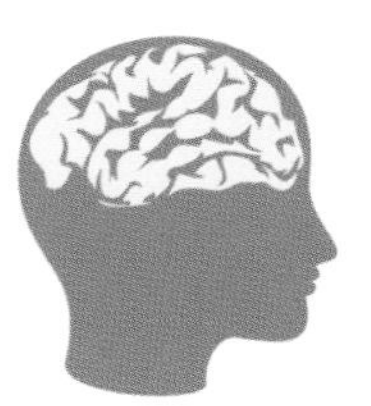

2

Valentina Tereshkova: First Woman in Space

Before humans entered space, we did not know how our body would react to it. In fact, animals were sent up into space before humans to make sure it was safe! The most famous of these were monkeys because their bodies are similar to our own. Once space flight was deemed safe, humans were sent up—but only men. We quickly learned how space travel affected men, but men and women are built differently. For us to know how women are affected, a female would need to go into space. Valentina Tereshkova is the first woman to have ever entered space, and her main job was to see how her body reacted to it.

Valentina Tereshkova was born on March 6, 1937, in Russia. She had not always dreamed of one day entering space. Instead, her first **passion** was parachuting and skydiving. She made her first jump at the age of twenty-two, and she became very good at it. At the same time, she worked in a textile factory.

Her experience as a skydiver, however, is what qualified her to become a cosmonaut. After the first male cosmonaut entered outer space, the Russian government decided to send a woman into space. Valentina Tereshkova was chosen just one year later. Along with her, four other women were chosen to train as cosmonauts. Lucky for Valentina, one of the requirements for being a cosmonaut was experience in skydiving! Her father was also a war hero who had died when she was two. This may have also helped the government choose her.

Astronauts and Cosmonauts

What is the difference between an astronaut and cosmonaut? Absolutely nothing! They are simply different words used by different countries to describe the same job. In the United States, a person who enters space is an astronaut. In Russia, he or she would be called a cosmonaut.

Training as a cosmonaut in Valentina's day was not much different from what it is today. She was prepared for weightlessness and isolation, and trained in engineering. Before takeoff, she was required to perform a minimum of 120 parachute jumps. This is because cosmonauts at the time were required to jump from their space shuttle and use a parachute to land safely on Earth's surface when they came out of orbit on their return from their mission.

Valentina entered space on June 16, 1963, in a spacecraft known as the Vostok 6. On this day, she made history as the first woman to enter space. Valentina spent about three days in space, orbiting the Earth forty-eight times. Up until that point, no one, not even men, had spent that much time in space.

What Valentina discovered was not much different from what happened to male cosmonauts. She felt a little sick to her stomach and uncomfortable, but she was fine otherwise. This proved that women could handle space just as well as men could.

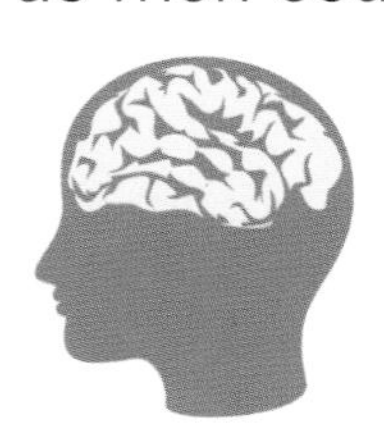

At the Gagarin Cosmonaut Training Center in Star City, Russia, NASA astronaut Catherine Coleman (right) had a chance to meet Valentina, the first woman to go into space.

When Valentina returned to Earth, the government asked her what she would like in return for her service. Valentina replied that she wanted to know where her father had died in war. The Russian government researched this, and a monument was placed in the city of his death.

Following her flight, Valentina chose to continue her education. She received a degree as a cosmonaut engineer from Zhukovsky Air Force Academy and eventually earned a PhD. (She did not have either of these degrees while on her record-setting flight.) After getting an education, Valentina became involved in the government. She was even awarded the Hero of the Soviet Union medal, the highest award that could be given to her at the time.

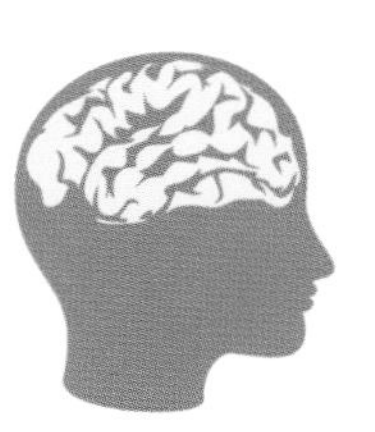

Today, Valentina is world famous as the first woman to enter space. She is a role model to women everywhere, but most especially to those in Russia. A crater on the moon is named after her. Although she has not entered space since her original flight, Valentina Tereshkova would not mind returning. She is especially interested in Mars and says she would like to travel there one day.

Words to Know

Passion: love for doing something.

Find Out More

GALE CENGAGE Learning, "Women's History: Valentina Tereshkova." www.gale.cengage.com/free_resources/whm/bio/tereshkova_v.htm

Russian Space Web, "News & History of Astronautics in the Former USSR" www.russianspaceweb.com/index.html

Sharpe, Mitchell R. *"It Is I, Sea Gull": Valentina Tereshkova, First Woman in Space*. New York: Crowell, 2005.

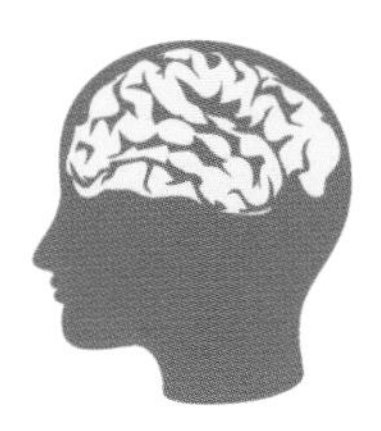

3

Sally Ride: First American Woman in Space

The first crew selected by NASA for space travel was made up of entirely men. This set the standard for what most Americans thought an astronaut could be. Sally Ride proved them wrong. She made history in 1983 when she became the first American woman to enter space. She was also the third female astronaut in the entire world. As the first female American astronaut, she became a role model for young women everywhere. She showed them that science was not strictly for men alone. A young girl could become an astronaut if she truly wanted to.

Sally Ride was born on May 26, 1951. As a girl, she was interested in many things, including science, English, and sports. She eventually became a high-ranking tennis player in the national junior tennis circuit. Her skills in tennis helped her attend a prep school in Los Angeles. As she reached the end of high school, she became very interested in physics. This interest continued with her to college.

Sally communicates with ground controllers from the flight deck during the six-day mission of the *Challenger.*

The college Sally Ride chose to attend was Swarthmore College in Pennsylvania. She studied physics there, but she left after deciding to pursue tennis as a career. When she changed her mind again, Sally went to Stanford University in California. From then on, she did not look back. She received a bachelor's degree in physics and English literature. Her master's degree and PhD were both in physics. Her area of expertise became **astrophysics** and electron laser physics. Sally completed her PhD in 1978.

Although she was selected to train as an astronaut in 1978, she did not enter space until five years later. Between training and entering space, she helped NASA on the ground. Her job was to communicate with the astronauts in space from the command center. These experiences helped her prepare for her launch in 1983. A year later, she entered into space again. As an engineer, she fixed complex problems on the shuttle and conducted experiments with a robotic arm.

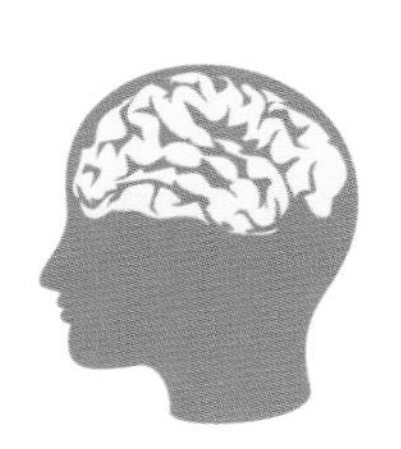

The Importance of Education

Being the first American woman in space gave Sally Ride an understanding of the pressures women face in the scientific world. Some people did not believe she could be a good astronaut because she was female. Others asked her offensive questions that implied a woman would not be able to emotionally handle the journey. Above all else, Sally Ride knew one thing: women in science are rare, and part of the reason is because of how they are treated. This is why Sally Ride began her own company, Sally Ride Science. Its purpose is to educate and inspire young people, especially women, to get involved in the sciences.

Sally Ride was also the first member of the LGBT community to be an astronaut. She had a female life partner for 27 years. On top of that, she became the youngest person from the United States to enter space, a record that has not yet been broken.

Sally Ride was preparing for a third departure into space when a tragedy occurred. In January of 1986, another spacecraft known as the Challenger exploded during takeoff. After this tragedy, Sally's job changed. She was chosen as part of a group of people to investigate the explosion and figure out what caused it. This group was known as the Rogers Commission.

In 1987, Sally Ride left NASA. She later became a professor of physics at University of California in San Diego. As she grew older, her strongest passion became educating young people. She believed science education in the United States was lacking compared to other countries. Her biggest goal was to make science exciting and engaging. Because she was already a role model for so many, this came naturally. She wrote several books about science for young people to read.

Sally Ride died in 2012. She is remembered by many as a **pioneer** in space science and education. Women look up to her as the youngest and first American female to ever enter space.

Words to Know

Astrophysics: a type of physics that focuses on studying stars and planets, and the rules that govern their behavior.
Pioneer: a person who is one of the first to come up with a new idea or conduct research in a new area.

Find Out More

Hurwitz, Jane, and Sue Hurwitz. *Sally Ride: Shooting for the Stars.* New York: Fawcett Columbine, 2009.

National Aeronautics and Space Administration,
"Biographical Data: Sally K. Ride."
www.jsc.nasa.gov/Bios/htmlbios/ride-sk.html

Ride, Sally, and Susan Okie. *To Space & Back*. New York: Beech Tree, 2001.

Sally Ride Science
www.sallyridescience.com

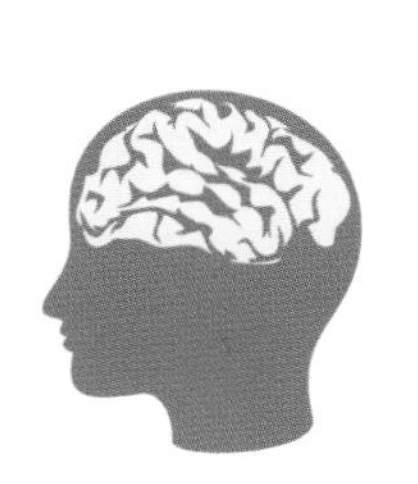

4

Shannon Lucid: NASA Chief Scientist

Astronauts have many areas of expertise. This is because astronauts need to fill many different roles while in space. Shannon Lucid is best known for her background in **biochemistry**. Her role in space was to perform experiments involving physical and life science.

Shannon Lucid was born on January 14, 1943 in China. Her family moved to the United States, and she grew up in Oklahoma. As a young girl, she loved the idea of exploration. At the same time, she was worried that one day there would be nothing left on Earth to explore. This is why she first became interested in space science. As far as we know, the universe is practically **infinite**, and there is always something new to learn!

Shannon attended the University of Oklahoma, where she eventually earned a PhD in biochemistry. Before joining NASA, she had a number of jobs. These

Shannon exercises on a treadmill during her time on the Russian space station.

included being a teaching assistant and laboratory technician. After completing her PhD in 1973, Shannon continued teaching and eventually applied to be an astronaut. In 1978, she was selected to begin training. Shannon was part of the very first group of female astronauts. This group included Sally Ride and four other women.

Unlike the other women in the group, Shannon Lucid was already a mother at the time of her selection. Sometimes, women are **discriminated** against because they are mothers. Some people believe a woman cannot hold a successful career if she has a child to take care of. NASA obviously did not believe this. All that mattered to NASA was Shannon's ability to do the job well. This is something she proved she was capable of time and time again.

Shannon first entered space in 1985, just two years after Sally Ride, the first American woman to enter space. She went on a number of short missions between 1985 and 1996. Many of these missions involved **deploying** some sort of

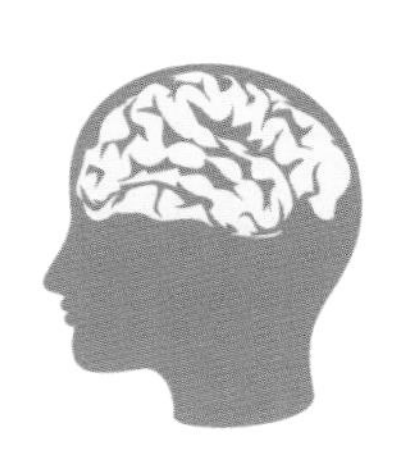

space shuttle or craft into space. One of these unmanned crafts traveled to Jupiter and studied the planet and its moons. As a researcher, Shannon performed experiments while on these missions. Her knowledge in biochemistry was useful for experiments in space.

Shannon is most famous for her fifth space flight in 1996. During this mission, she spent time on the Russian space station, *Mir*. She spent a total of 188 days in space during this mission, with 179 of those days spent on *Mir*. She was originally supposed to come back to the Earth much sooner, but her return was delayed. This meant she made a new record for the most time spent in space by a woman. She held this record until 2007 when it was broken by Sunita Williams. Shannon Lucid still holds the record for longest time spent by an American on the Russian Space Station, *Mir*.

In 2002, Shannon became the Chief Scientist of NASA. This is the highest position a scientist can hold at this organization. The Chief Scientist is in charge of overseeing scientific advancements and research. In 2005, she became a

The Importance of a Ground Crew

When we think of NASA, we often think about the astronauts in space, but most of NASA's crew is on the ground. The ground crew is just as important as the astronauts in the sky. Mission Control helps astronauts control their space craft, perform experiments, and plan for the future. A member of the ground crew could be a retired astronaut or someone who hopes to one day become an astronaut. Some members of the ground crew have no desire to enter space. Instead, they prefer to make advancements in space science from the surface of the Earth.

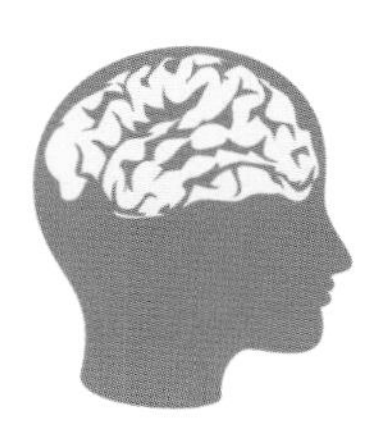

capsule communicator, or CAPCOM. The capsule communicator is one of the only people who communicates directly with a crew in space. Because there always needs to be someone available to talk with the space crew, there is often more than one CAPCOM. Shannon had the overnight shift.

Shannon Lucid was awarded the Congressional Space Medal of Honor in 1996. She held her position as a capsule communicator until she announced her retirement in 2012. Shannon is the tenth person and first woman to receive this honor. Her curiosity first brought her into space science—but it was her dedication that helped her succeed.

Words to Know

Biochemistry: a science that deals with the substances that make up living things.
Infinite: limitless; impossible to measure or find the end of.
Discriminated: to be unfairly judged because of one's social identity, such as gender, religion, ethnicity, or sexual orientation.
Deploying: bringing into action

Find Out More

Bredeson, Carmen. *Shannon Lucid: Space Ambassador*. Brookfield, Conn.: Millbrook, 2008.

National Aeronautics and Space Administration,
"Biographical Data: Shannon W. Lucid"
www.jsc.nasa.gov/Bios/htmlbios/lucid.html

National Aeronautics and Space Administration,
"NASA-2 Shannon Lucid: Enduring Qualities"
history.nasa.gov/SP-4225/nasa2/nasa2.htm

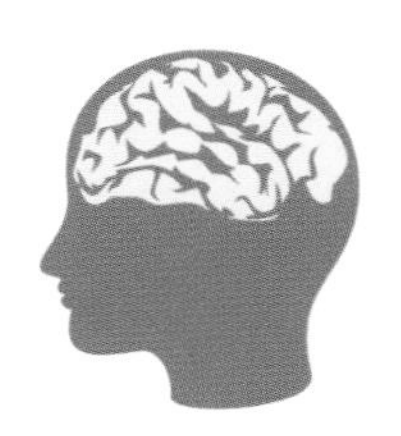

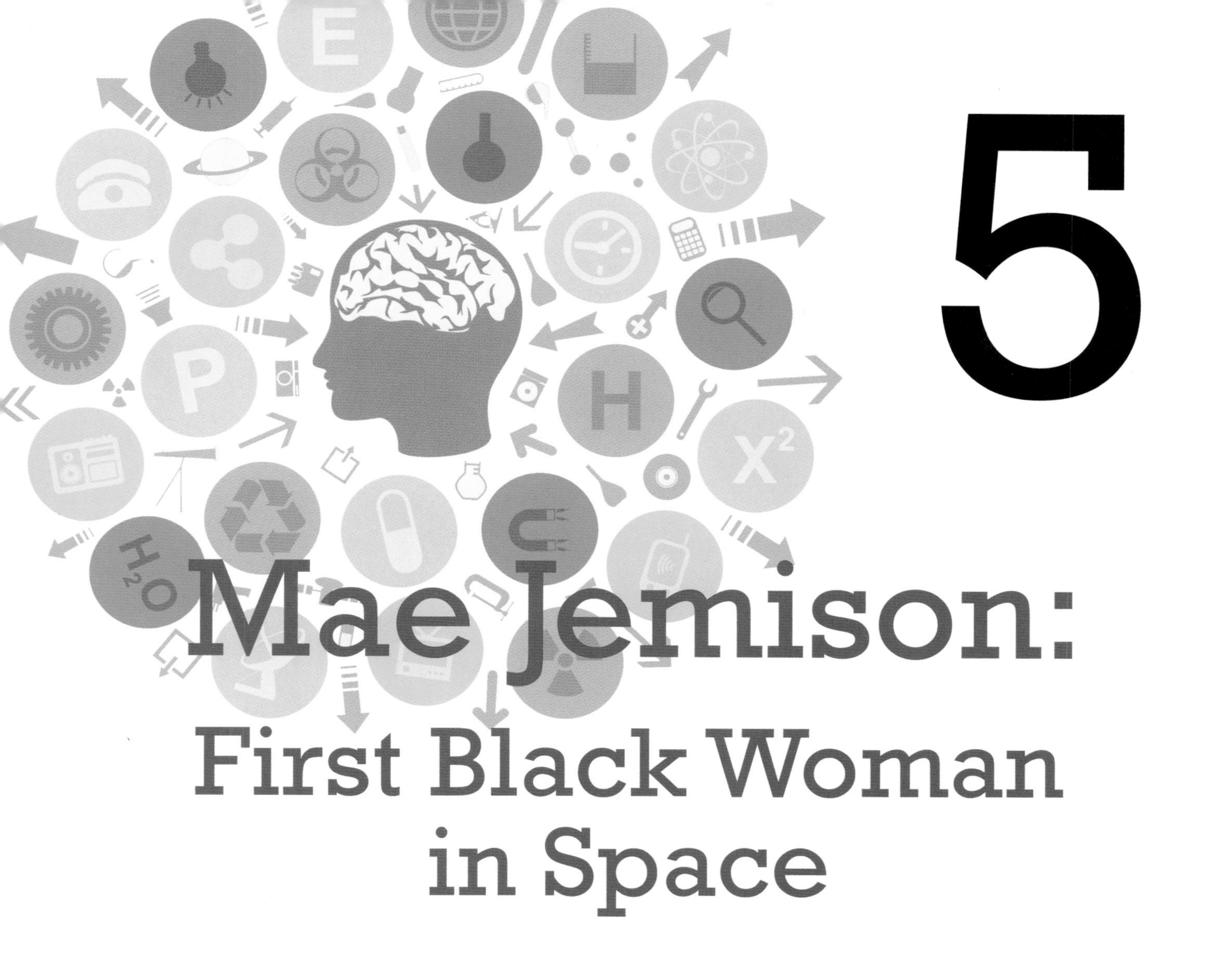

5

Mae Jemison: First Black Woman in Space

History was forever changed when Mae Jemison became the first black woman to travel into space in 1992. Her career route was very different from other astronauts'. Before being accepted by NASA, she was a physician and member of the Peace Corps. Her medical background made her an ideal **candidate** for a space flight.

Mae was born on October 17, 1956 in Alabama. When she was three years old, her family moved to Chicago, Illinois. Her fascination with space began at a young age. Because space exploration was already happening, she assumed a lot more people would be traveling into space by the time she was an adult. This didn't happen—but it did not prevent Mae from following her dream!

Mae at work on board the space lab in 2010.

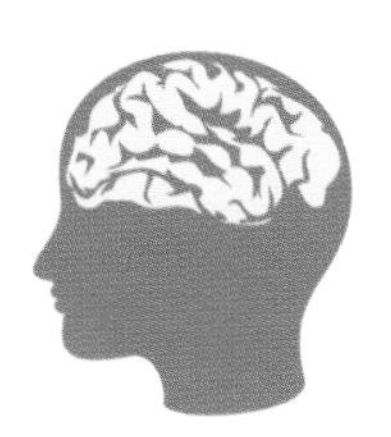

Mae was always interested in science. The natural world fascinated her. She loved art as well, and especially dancing. Although she had many other interests, Mae also did very well in school. In fact, she entered Stanford University when she was only sixteen! She graduated in 1977 after earning a bachelor's degree. The two majors she studied—chemical engineering and African and African American studies—were very different from one another, proving the breadth of her interests.

In 1981, Mae earned an MD from Cornell Medical College. Next she became an **intern** at a medical center, and after that, a general practitioner. (A general practitioner might also be called a family doctor.)

Mae was a very **compassionate** person. She liked to travel and help people in other countries. From 1983 to 1985, she was a member of the Peace Corps, using her medical degree to help people in other countries.

When Sally Ride became the first American woman to enter space, Mae was inspired. She felt as if any woman could become an astronaut now that Sally Ride had. She decided to apply to NASA's astronaut program. It took several years, but Mae was finally accepted into the program in 1987. In 1992, she went into space as a mission specialist.

Racial Pressures

Being a female scientist was already hard enough. Being a black female scientist was even harder! When Mae Jemison was studying engineering, she found it very hard to be taken seriously in a scientific field. Mae dealt with discrimination from both her peers and her professors. She did not let this stop her, however. She wanted to be a scientist, and she didn't care how hard it was to get there!

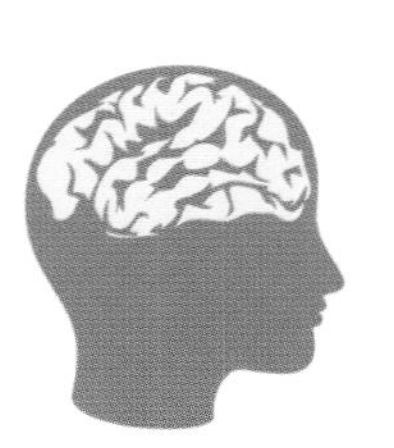

Mae spent just over a week in space. To her, this was an accomplishment of a lifetime. As a young girl, she had dreamed of going into space—and now she had made that happen through hard work and dedication.

The year after her first space mission, Mae Jemison retired from NASA. She chose to start her own company next. She has also taught as a professor at Cornell University and Dartmouth College. In 1992, she was inducted into the National Women's Hall of Fame, and she was added to the International Space Hall of Fame in 2004.

Today, she continues to support the importance of women and minorities in science. She is a role model for women everywhere, proving just how far women can go.

Words to Know

Candidate: a person or thing well-suited for a particular job or task.
Intern: a recent medical school graduate who is receiving training at a hospital or medical facility.
Compassionate: showing sympathy and concern for living things, including other people.

Find Out More

Black, Sonia. *Mae Jemison*. New York: Mondo, 2000.

Dr. Mae: Daring Makes a Difference
www.drmae.com

National Aeronautics and Space Administration,
"Biographical Data: Mae. C Jemison"
www.jsc.nasa.gov/Bios/htmlbios/jemison-mc.html

6

Kalpana Chawla: From India to Space

Not all countries have space programs. The ones that do may not be as advanced as NASA. In order to become an astronaut, Kalpana Chawla needed to travel from her home in India to the United States. There, she became the first Indian woman to enter space.

When Kalpana was born in 1961, female scientists were not common or respected in India. According to her mother, however, Kalpana was very independent and unique for her age and gender. She learned karate, cut her own hair, and did not wear ironed clothes. In addition to science, she also loved art and reading about famous artists.

Even as a child, Kalpana had a love for flying and an interest in space. She wanted to one day become a pilot. When she told her parents of her desire to

Kalpana on *Columbia*'s flight deck.

train as a pilot, however, her father discouraged her. A male professor even told her that being an engineer was not "ladylike."

Although many people discouraged her, Kalpana did not let this stop her. She earned a bachelor's degree in aerospace engineering from Punjab Engineering College in 1982. She became the first female to join this university's aeronautical engineering program. Even with this degree, people still discouraged her from becoming a pilot. It was clear to her that she would need to go elsewhere to fulfill her dreams.

A Dangerous Job

Space travel is still very new. Anything can happen when an astronaut goes into space. All astronauts must be prepared for this. NASA spends a long time researching how to make a space flight as safe as possible, but accidents can still happen. Not every astronaut faces such a tragic end as Kalpana and her fellow crew members, but all astronauts put their lives on the line in the name of science.

When Kalpana wanted to continue her education in the United States, her father had a change of heart. He decided to help her travel to the United States and complete her education. She attended the University of Texas and completed a master's degree in aeronautical engineering just two years later, in 1984. In the United States, she also met her future husband, Jean Pierre Harrison. He introduced her to many new hobbies, including scuba diving, hiking, and most important, flying. He was a flying instructor and could help her finally achieve her dream.

After earning her PhD from the University of Colorado, Kalpana began working for NASA. She studied how air flowed around a spacecraft as it traveled to and from space. Kalpana also began working at Overset Methods, Inc., and became the vice president of this company.

When Kalpana applied to become an astronaut, she did not expect to get in. But she did! In 1994, she was accepted into the program and, in 1995, she began training. At only 5 feet tall and 90 pounds, she did not fit inside a standard space suit. When she did go to space, she was required to work inside the space shuttle at all times. She was too light to go outside.

After two years of training, Kalpana entered space in 1997 on the Space Shuttle *Columbia* flight STS-87. At the time, she had many duties, including controlling a robotic arm. The purpose of the studies during this flight was to better understand how weightlessness affected people and objects. The crew also

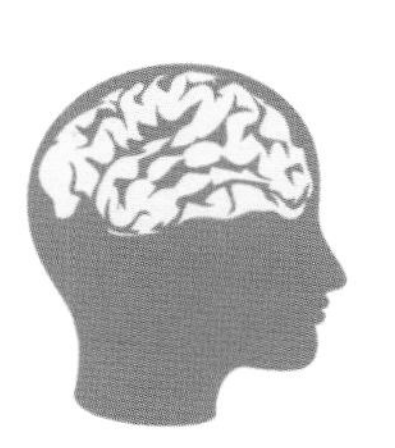

studied the atmospheric layers of the sun. Because the Earth's atmosphere acts as a shield from the sun, the sun is best studied from space.

Kalpana loved her first trip in space and was delighted when she was chosen for a second one. The new Space *Columbia* Flight was STS-107. The flight was delayed for a long time because of technical issues, but it finally went into space on January 16, 2003. When it returned on February 1, 2003, a terrible accident happened. The entire crew of the space shuttle, including Kalpana, died that day as the shuttle was reentering the atmosphere.

Today, Kalpana is remembered as an inspiration to women. Although she was a part of NASA, she is also remembered in India. One of India's space shuttles, the *Kalpana-1*, is named in her honor. Features within space have also been named after her, such as a hill on Mars and a star in deep space. Her courage and intelligence will never be forgotten.

Find Out More

Cole, Michael D., and Michael D. Cole. *The Columbia Space Shuttle Disaster: From First Liftoff to Tragic Final Fligh*t. Berkeley Heights, N.J.: Enslow, 2003.

Harisson, Jean-Pierre. *The Edge of Time: The Authoritative Biography of Kalpana Chawla*. Los Gatos, Calif.: Harisson, 2011.

National Aeronautics and Space Administration,
"Biographical Data: Kalpana Chawla"
www.jsc.nasa.gov/Bios/htmlbios/chawla.html

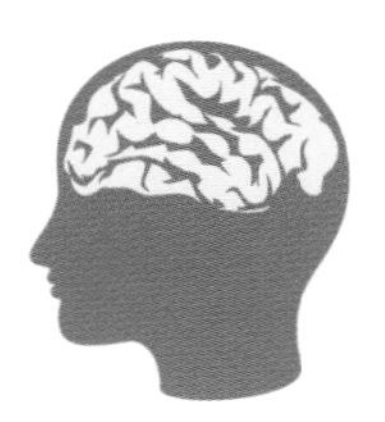

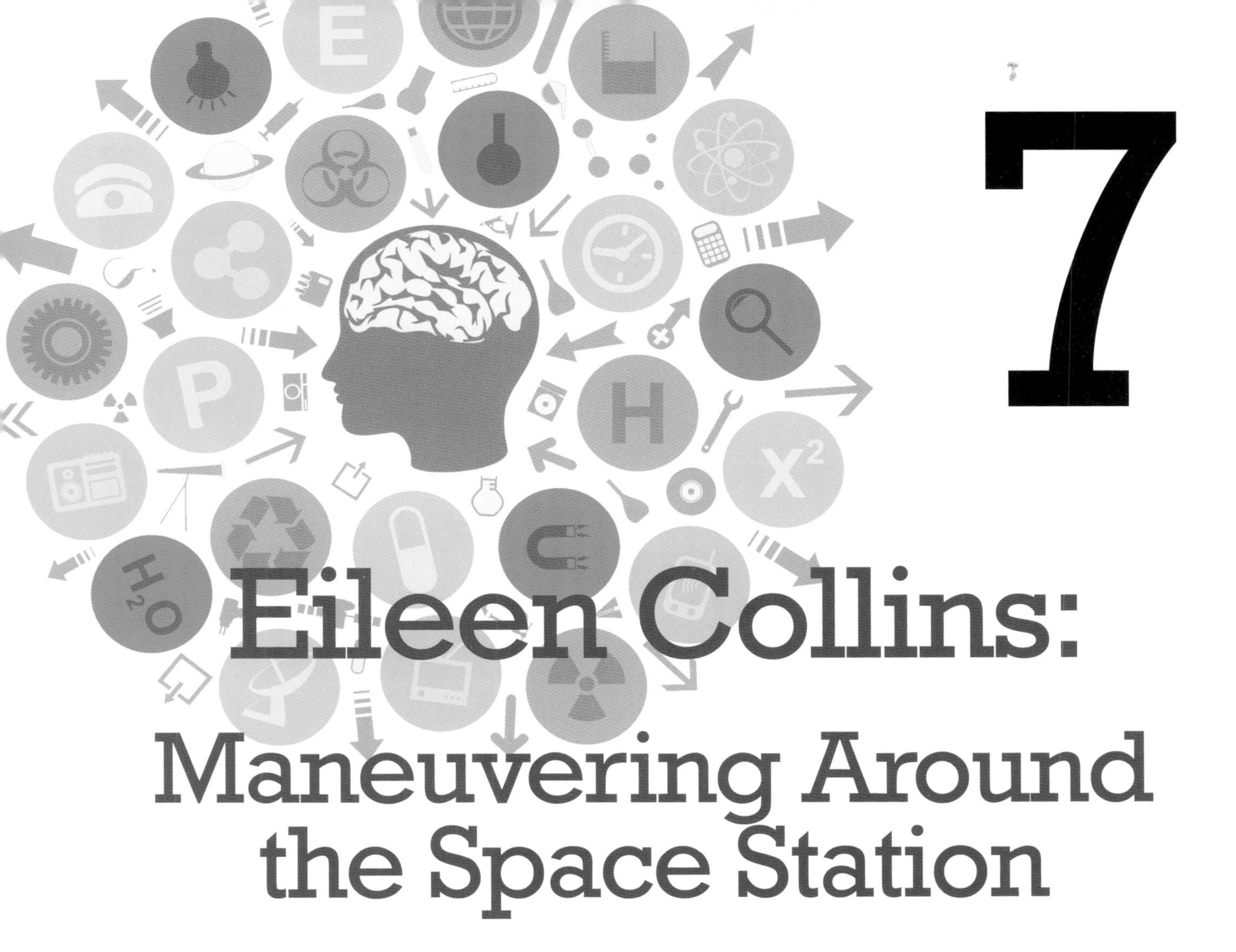

7

Eileen Collins: Maneuvering Around the Space Station

Before joining NASA, Eileen Collins was a military instructor and test pilot. This flying experience led to her becoming the first female pilot and commander of a space shuttle. Eileen was born on November 19, 1956. Even as a young girl, she knew she wanted to become a pilot one day. Female pilots were not common when she was young, but she didn't care. She wanted to be one, and she wasn't going to let anything stop her. Eileen was also interested in space travel, but she did not pursue this until much later.

Before becoming a pilot, Eileen knew she needed a strong education. She earned a bachelor's degree in mathematics and **economics** from Syracuse University in 1978. After college, she chose to join a pilot-training course at Oklahoma's Vance Air Force Base. The class she was in was one of the first to train

Eileen Collins consults a checklist while seated in the flight deck commander's seat.

women at this location. After completing the course in 1979, she became an instructor for other pilots in training.

Three years later, she was transferred to the Travis Air Force Base in California. She helped with military missions by flying cargo planes. These planes helped carry equipment and supplies from one area to another. She also enrolled at Stanford University and earned a master's degree in **operations research** in 1986. She earned another master's degree, this time from Webster University, three years later. This master's degree was in space systems management.

With her newfound education and experience as a pilot, she was ready to become an astronaut. NASA selected her for training in 1990. Five years later, she became the first woman to pilot a space shuttle mission. Although not yet a commander, she was second-in-command. The mission, which occurred in 1995, was a success. Eileen proved she had what it takes.

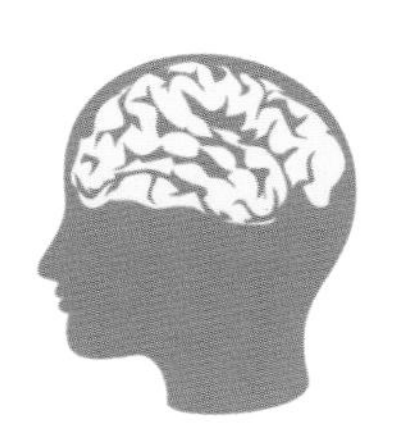

Finding Time for Family

Eileen is an astronaut who proves that women can be both leaders in their fields and mothers. Between her first and second flight into space, she took time off to give birth to her daughter. She participated in her next mission only a year after giving birth.

Eileen returned to space several times. In 1999, she was the commander of the shuttle she piloted. The object of this mission was to put a very expensive telescope into orbit. The telescope was worth over 1.5 billion dollars! This satellite, known as the Chandra X-ray Observatory, collects and analyzes X-ray data.

In 2003, after Kalpana Chawla and her crew members were killed while returning to Earth, NASA needed to understand why the terrible accident had happened before it could send any more missions into space. Eventually, NASA determined that the shuttle was damaged during takeoff. The ground crew had not realized it was damaged because they could not see the problem from Earth. Specialists on the ground needed to think of a way to prevent this from happening in the future. They thought long and hard and finally came up with a solution.

In 2005, Eileen returned to space once again. This mission, the first after the tragic 2003 mission, was to bring supplies to the International Space Station. At the time, the International Space Station was full of other astronauts. When Eileen met up with the International Space Station, she needed to turn the ship so that the astronauts on the space station could see its underside. These astronauts would then take pictures and send the images to NASA to analyze. They would be able to see if there was any damage to the shuttle.

Performing this maneuver so close to the International Space Station was very risky because it had never been done before. Eileen was the first pilot to perform it. Today, turning a shuttle that enters space to check for damage is standard procedure. All shuttles must perform this maneuver in front of the International Space Station before returning to Earth. A major accident like the one in 2003 has not happened since.

The International Space Station

For a long time, different countries worked alone in their mission to study and visit space. The most notable of these are the United States and Russia. Today, different countries know it is best to work together in our pursuit of knowledge. The International Space Station is how we do that. It is the largest satellite in orbit and has been inhabited for over a decade.

How did we get something so big into space in the first place? Over time. More and more pieces of the space station are still being launched into space and connected to the satellite that is already there. Five organizations that contribute are NASA (United States), RKA (Russia), JAXA (Japan), ESA (Europe), and CSA (Canada). These countries help fund the projects and send trained astronauts to the space station.

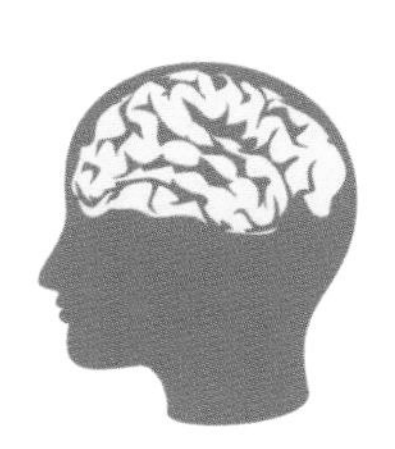

Eileen Collins retired in 2006. Although she was still interested in space travel, she wanted to take some time to herself to pursue other interests. She can still be seen on television giving interviews and advice about space travel. She is an inspiration to many young women.

Words to Know

Economics: the study of the production, use, and distribution of wealth and other resources such as time.

Operations research: the use of scientific and mathematical principles to help make better decisions.

Find Out More

National Aeronautics and Space Administration,
"Biographical Data: Eileen Marie Collins"
www.jsc.nasa.gov/Bios/htmlbios/collins.html

Raum, Elizabeth. *Eileen Collins*. Chicago, Illinois: Heinemann Library, 2006.

Space.com, "NASA's First Female Shuttle Commander Retires from Spaceflight"
www.space.com/2360-nasa-female-shuttle-commander-retires-spaceflight.html

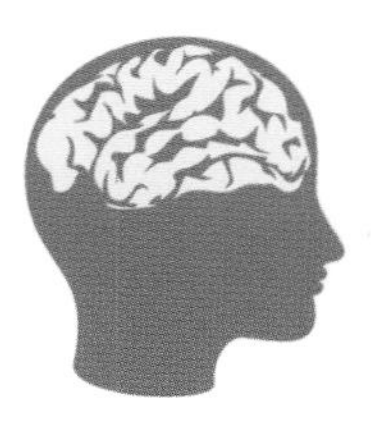

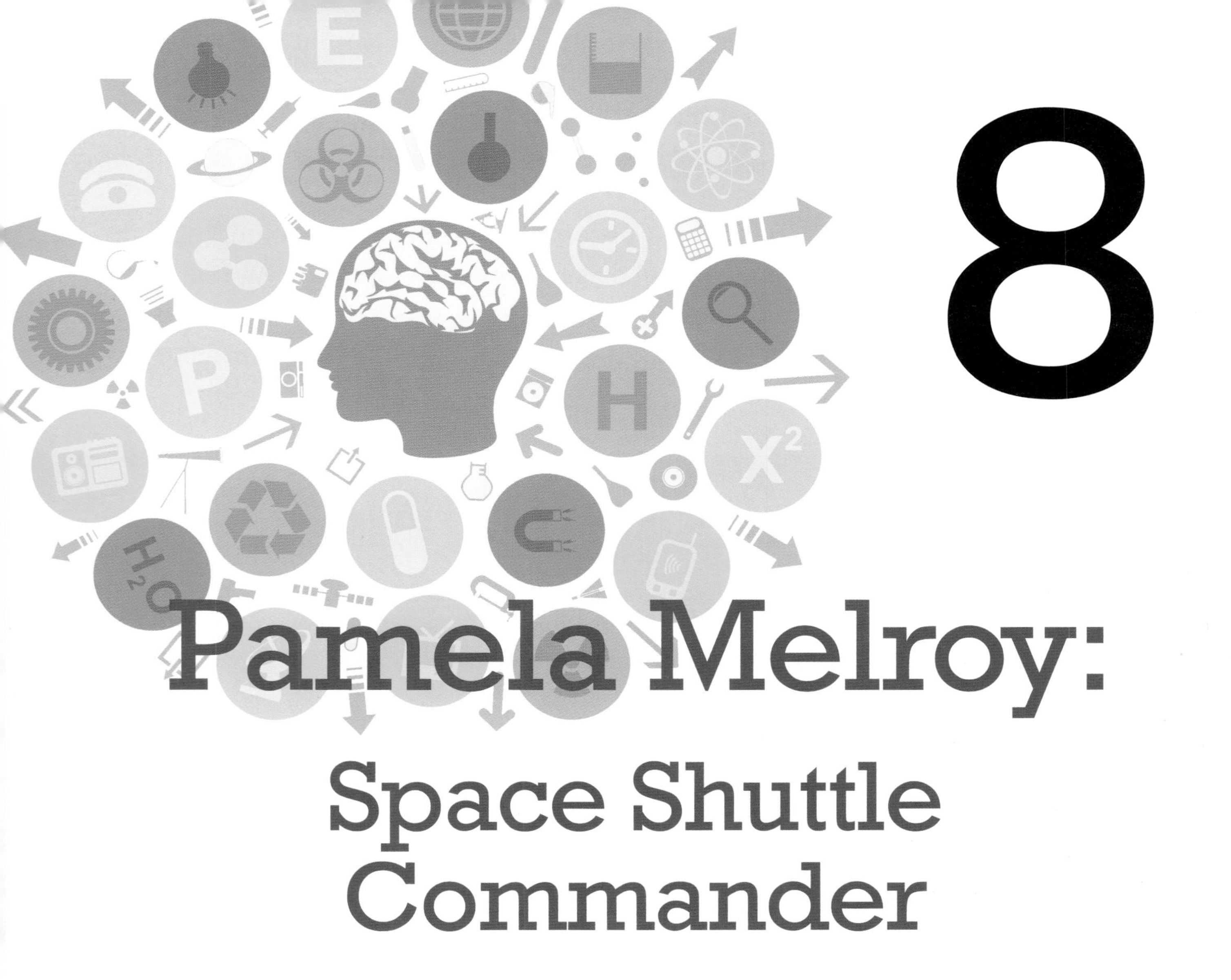

8

Pamela Melroy: Space Shuttle Commander

Being a pilot can sometimes lead to being an astronaut. That's how it worked for Pamela Melroy.

Pamela was born on September 17, 1961 in California. She grew up in Rochester, New York, and she was always interested in flying. She graduated from Wellesley College in 1983 with a degree in physics and astronomy. (Physicists study how objects move and interact while astronomers study space.) Pamela went on to the Massachusetts Institute of Technology (MIT) and graduated in 1984. There, she combined her favorite areas of study and earned a master's degree in earth and planetary sciences.

After college, Pamela joined the military and began training as a pilot at the Reese Air Force Base. Her understanding of physics helped her with her training. She worked as a copilot, aircraft commander, and instructor. She also served overseas and was a veteran of several battles. These included the operations of Just Cause, Desert Shield, and Desert Storm. She has spent over 200 hours in combat or supporting combat.

After serving in the military, Pamela became a **test pilot**. She ended up with over 5,000 hours of flight time in a total of several dozen aircrafts. All this experience made her a good candidate for NASA, and she was selected as an astronaut in 1994. Now, in addition to being an astronaut, she helped advise fellow astronauts from the ground.

Making History Together

During Pamela Melroy's third journey into space in 2007, she was the mission commander of her space shuttle. This made her the second woman to have ever commanded a shuttle mission. (The first was Eileen Collins.) While in space, Pamela's shuttle met up with the International Space Station, where at the time, Peggy Whitson was the commander. For the first time, two women commanders were in orbit at the same time.

Pamela's main job as astronaut was piloting the spacecraft. Her first flight was in 2000, and her second was in 2002. On her third, in 2007, she became the mission commander. All three of her missions involved delivering supplies and equipment to the International Space Station. The supplies provided food for the astronauts, while the equipment allowed the space station to grow larger and more advanced.

Each of Pamela's missions was very successful. On the first, her crew helped prepare the International Space Station to use solar power. A truss, or large metal piece, was attached to the top of the Space Station. A separate crew would bring the actual solar panels to space and attach them. A secondary dock was also attached to the International Space Station to create a second entrance where space shuttles could land. Her second and third missions brought more

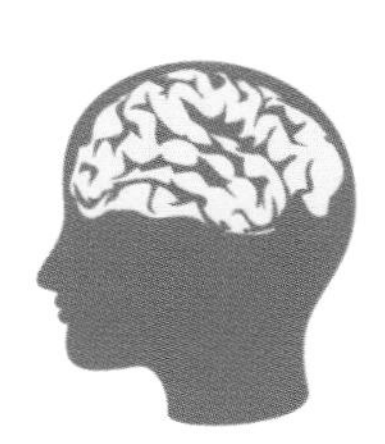

pieces to the International Space Station. While on her second mission, Pamela, from inside the ship, guided astronauts performing a space walk.

Pamela Melroy chose to retire from the Air Force in 2007, the same year she completed her last mission into space. Two years later, she also decided to leave NASA, after serving fourteen years as a member of the NASA team.

She believes that even though only some people get chosen to train and eventually go to space, everyone on Earth is a part of this grand endeavor. Whether or not they ever reach space themselves, women everywhere can learn and be inspired by Pamela's life.

Words to Know

Test pilot: a person who flies new planes to check how well they perform.

Find Out More

National Aeronautics and Space Administration,
"Biographical Data: Pamela Ann Melroy"
www.jsc.nasa.gov/Bios/htmlbios/melroy.html

The Ninety-Nines, Inc., "Pamela Melroy: Ready for Flight"
www.ninety-nines.org/index.cfm/pamela_melroy.htm

Space.com, "Female Space Commanders Set for Landmark Mission"
www.space.com/4339-female-space-commanders-set-landmark-mission.html

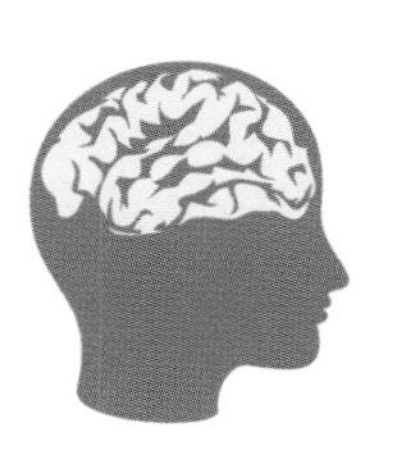

PEGGY WHITSON

9

Peggy Whitson: International Space Station Commander

By the time Peggy Whitson became an astronaut, plenty of women had already been to space. However, none of them had commanded a mission before. Not only did Peggy become a commander, but she commanded the International Space Station. She is also a record-setter in another way. Currently, she has spent over 376 days in space. That's over a year! This is longer than any other female astronaut, making her the most experienced.

Peggy Whitson was born on a farm in a rural town in Iowa on February 9, 1960. She went to Wesleyan College and graduated with a bachelor of science degree in biology and chemistry. Then Peggy continued her education at Rice University, where she earned a PhD in biochemistry. She stayed at the university doing research until she went to work for the Johnson Space Center in Texas and began working for NASA.

Peggy with Pam Melroy onboard the space station.

Her background as a biochemist was useful in the work she did for NASA. Although she was not yet an astronaut herself, Peggy helped do research to prepare other astronauts for the work they would do in space. This included important scientific experiments. During this time, she also became an assistant professor at Rice University, specializing in biochemical and **genetic engineering**. Peggy gradually rose in rank and responsibility until she was well respected in her field.

In 1996, Peggy was finally selected as an astronaut candidate. First, however, she had to be trained to lead. Years went by before she could actually go into space—but when she did, her first stay upon the space station lasted six months, much longer than most of the astronauts that came before her had ever stayed there. One of her duties included installing a mobile base system. She even performed a space walk to install shielding outside of the craft.

During this mission to the International Space Station, Peggy was named the first science officer. She oversaw what other astronauts did and the experiments that were performed. It was her job to make sure the astronauts stuck to schedule and finished everything they needed to do before returning home.

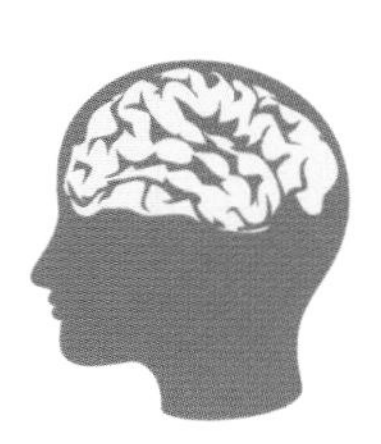

In 2007, Peggy returned to space again. She stayed for about the same amount of time as her first voyage. During this second flight, Peggy Whitson became the first female commander of the space station. She performed five spacewalks to help maintain the outside of the station. After returning to Earth, she became the first female Chief of the Astronaut Office. She held this position from 2009 until 2012, when she chose to step down. Peggy is still a member of NASA, however, and could be chosen to perform another flight into space.

As a woman, Peggy forged ahead and set many records. She was the first female commander; she holds the record as the female astronaut with the most time spent on space walks; and her total time in space, over a year, makes her the female with the most time in space. She shows us that women can truly reach the stars.

Words to Know

Genetic engineering: the science of changing living things by manipulating their DNA.

Find Out More

Baker, David. *International Space Station 1998–2011 (All Stages): Owners' Workshop Manual.* Sparkford: Haynes, 2012.

National Aeronautics and Space Administration,
"Biographical Data: Peggy Whitson"
www.jsc.nasa.gov/Bios/htmlbios/whitson.html

National Aeronautics and Space Administration, "Expedition Five: Letters Hope #1"
spaceflight.nasa.gov/station/crew/exp5/lettershome1.html

Universe Today, "Peggy Whitson: A Heroine of Science and Technology."
www.universetoday.com/60656/peggy-whitson-a-heroine-of-science-and-technology

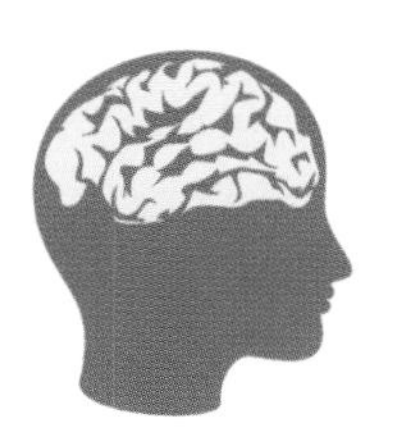

10

Rose Grymes: Astrobiologist

Not everyone that works for NASA travels into space. In fact, only a handful of people become astronauts. Some scientists contribute just as much to our understanding of space from the ground. Rose Grymes is one of those scientists. She has held many positions at NASA, where she has helped with research and education. Today, she continues to do research to help NASA develop its programs.

Rose Grymes has always been interested in biology on a small scale. This is known as microbiology. Microbiologists examine very small living things, such as cells. Cells are the building blocks of life and cannot be seen without a microscope.

The NASA Astrobiology Institute

Who do you think comes up with the experiments that astronauts are told to perform in space? Chances are, the Astrobiology Institute had something to do with it! Astrobiology is the study of how organisms and planets interact. Some of the institute's most interesting projects involve the search for life in outer space. Astrobiologists are most interested in how life evolves and changes over time. If one day we are ever unable to live on Earth, astrobiologists may be the ones in charge of finding us a new planet to live!

Rose earned a bachelor's degree in **virology** from the University of California. Virologists look at viruses and what causes them. With this knowledge, we can find ways to fight viruses that can make humans very sick.

In 1983, Rose earned a PhD from Stanford University. Her major was cancer biology, and her minor was medical microbiology. After having a daughter, she decided to go back to work in medical research. Soon after, in 1991, she joined NASA.

One of Rose's earliest jobs was helping with outreach programs. These programs are meant to educate the public about what NASA does and discovers. Outreach programs also explain why what NASA does is so important. Another role Rose had was as part of the Astrobiology Institute. Astrobiologists are concerned with living things and how they are affected by space.

NASA has several research centers throughout the United States. Rose joined NASA's Ames Research Center in California in 1991. The research done at these centers is very important because it helps us plan for the space missions of the future.

Another of Rose's passions is education. In addition to her research at NASA, she has also become the library commissioner of the City of Cupertino, where she finds ways to help people of all ages have access to information.

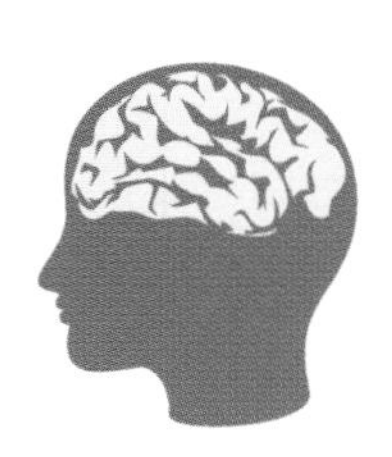

As a scientist, Rose understands better than anyone how humans are affecting the environment, and because of this, she became a GSA Sustainability Fellow in 2012. These scientists find ways to reduce the negative impacts humans have on the planet. A scientist studying **sustainability** might try to find materials that are less harmful to the environment—which can then be used to make the spaceships and satellites of the future.

Rose understands the challenges many women face in scientific fields. In order to overcome these challenges, she suggests finding a **mentor**.

Rose Gryme's life proves that if she could do it, so can other women!

Words to Know

Virology: the study of viruses, microscopic agents that infect living things and make them sick.

Sustainability: the ability to maintain something, specifically the ability for natural processes such as weather patterns to remain consistent.

Mentor: a trusted adviser who forms a close relationship with his or her students.

Find Out More

National Aeronautics and Space Administration,
"Astrobiology: Life in the Universe"
astrobiology.nasa.gov

Welcome to NASA Quest, "Meet: Rosalind A. Grymes"
quest.nasa.gov/neuron/team/grymes.html

Welcome to NASA Quest, "Quest Astrobiology Chat Featuring: Dr. Rose Grymes"
quest.arc.nasa.gov/projects/astrobiology/chats/11-02-01rg.html

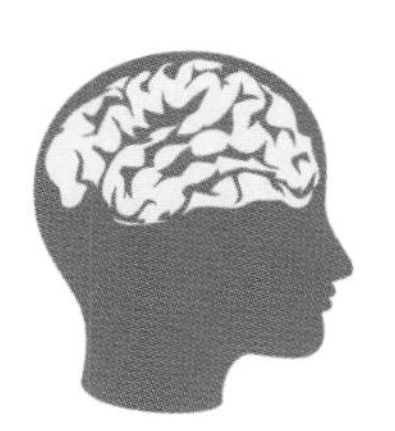

NASA

11

Opportunities for Women in Space

Thanks to the female astronauts of yesterday, becoming a woman in space is not as hard as it used to be. What you will do in space depends on what you have to offer NASA. You might be an astronaut who actually travels into space. Or you might study space from the ground. Some astronauts perform experiments, while others build and maintain the equipment. Pilots are needed to control spacecraft. Even if you are not chosen to be one of the lucky few who gets to leave the Earth, you can still help with space research as a scientist on the ground. Many astronauts were once part of the ground crew before being chosen for training.

Kathie Olsen is NASA's Chief Scientist. Here she shows public school teachers around NASA's Glenn Research Center.

Research Scientists

A huge part of our research in space is figuring out what makes it different from Earth. How does low gravity affect people, plants, and other organisms? How does it alter physics as we know it? Scientists that are experts at these things on Earth are the best to conduct the experiments in space.

Research scientists are often the first to make a discovery about space. They have the opportunity to share it with the world. Research scientists can use their experience to help think up new experiments that should be performed in the future. In this way, they are always helping to improve space science and keep it

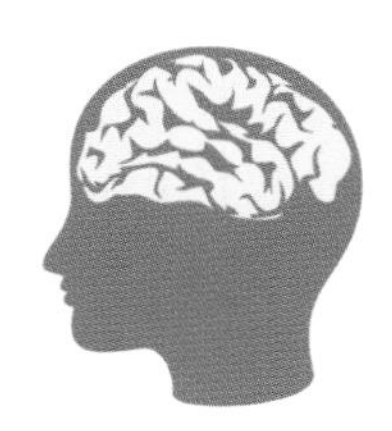

moving forward. Some argue that research scientists are actually the most important type of astronaut.

Engineers

Space shuttles have a lot of equipment. The International Space Station has even more! Engineers help maintain this equipment and keep it safe. If it **malfunctions** while in space, it is up to engineers to fix it. The equipment is very expensive and simply replacing it is not an option. Besides, if you're up in space when something breaks, you can't just send out for a replacement!

One of NASA's engineers at work.

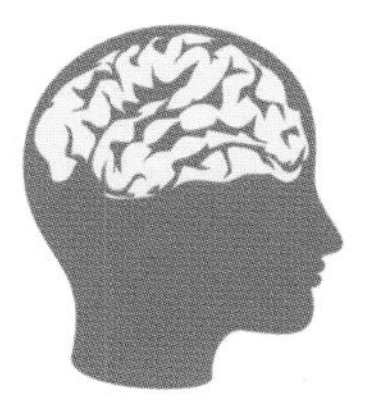

NASA's ground crew directs science operations, sends commands to the spacecraft, receives data from experiments aboard the Space Shuttle, adjusts mission schedules to take advantage of unexpected science opportunities or unexpected results, and works with crew members to resolve problems with their experiments.

Many engineers help invent new equipment that will be used by astronauts. They might also develop probes that are sent to destinations where an astronaut cannot go yet. One example is Mars. Because humans cannot yet travel there, engineers needed to develop complex tools and machines that could function on their own. Several rovers have been sent to Mars, with the most recent being *Curiosity*. It landed in 2012 and continues to send us information about the Red Planet. Without engineers, this feat would not have been possible.

Pilots

Someone has to steer and guide a spaceship. This person is a pilot. Pilots begin their training on standard airplanes. They must be very experienced before even

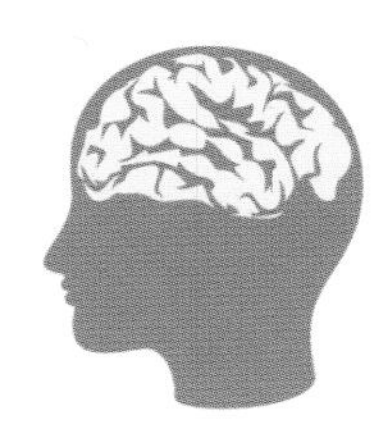

being considered by NASA. If NASA chooses them, they are then trained to control and monitor spacecrafts. They will also go through the same training as all other astronauts.

Controlling a shuttle in space is very different from controlling a plane. This is why space pilots often train using simulators.

Pilots are also very important during landing. Not everything can be controlled from the ground, and landing on the Earth is a very tricky process because the shuttle moves very fast as it reenters Earth's atmosphere. If the shuttle is damaged in some way, the landing must be altered. The pilot holds the lives of everyone on board in her hands.

On the Ground

The ground crew is very important. They may not be as famous as astronauts, but they are crucial to the success of any mission.

Even though astronauts might feel isolated when they are so many miles above the Earth, they know that help is always available from the ground. NASA staff help to solve problems and make sure a mission is running smoothly. They also help with takeoff and landing. A crew of astronauts in space must keep in constant contact with the crew on the ground. After an astronaut has finished her mission in space, she might continue to work as a member of the ground crew.

Other Opportunities for a Career in Space

NASA may be the route to taking off into orbit—but there are plenty of other careers in space science. Scientists work with the Hubble Space Telescope and the James Webb Telescope, empowering the entire astronomy community to produce new scientific discoveries, while bringing the benefits of this research to the public. This kind of work promotes new space missions with the potential for unlocking the secrets of the universe. The military and the defense industry also offer opportunities for people who are interested in space.

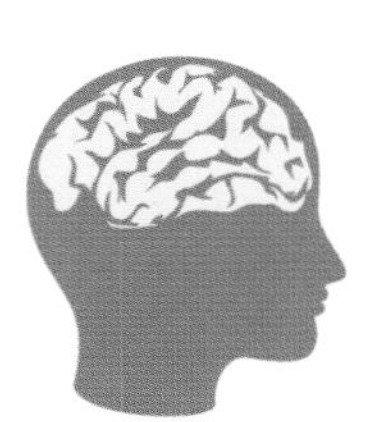

Engineers

While the astronauts who travel to outer space are the ones who get most of the public's attention, the engineers on the ground are the people who make space exploration travel possible. They design spacecrafts, space vehicles, space stations, and the space satellites that help us better understand the weather and climate conditions that impact our daily lives. There are opportunities for many different types of engineers in the field of space science, including:

- aerospace or aeronautical engineers
- **avionics** and instrumentation engineers
- computer engineers
- materials engineers
- mechanical engineers
- robotics engineers
- spacecraft engineers
- telecommunications engineers

Scientists

Many scientists choose to pursue **research-and-development** careers in space science. For example, **pharmacology** researchers are investigating ways to develop new medications from substances discovered during space exploration trips. There are opportunities in space science for scientists who specialize in a wide variety of fields, including:

- astrophysicists
- biologists
- chemists
- **geologists**
- medical doctors
- **meteorologists**
- physicists

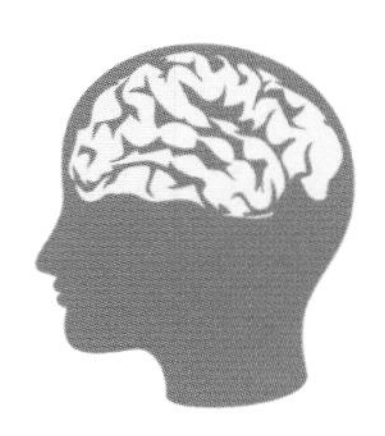

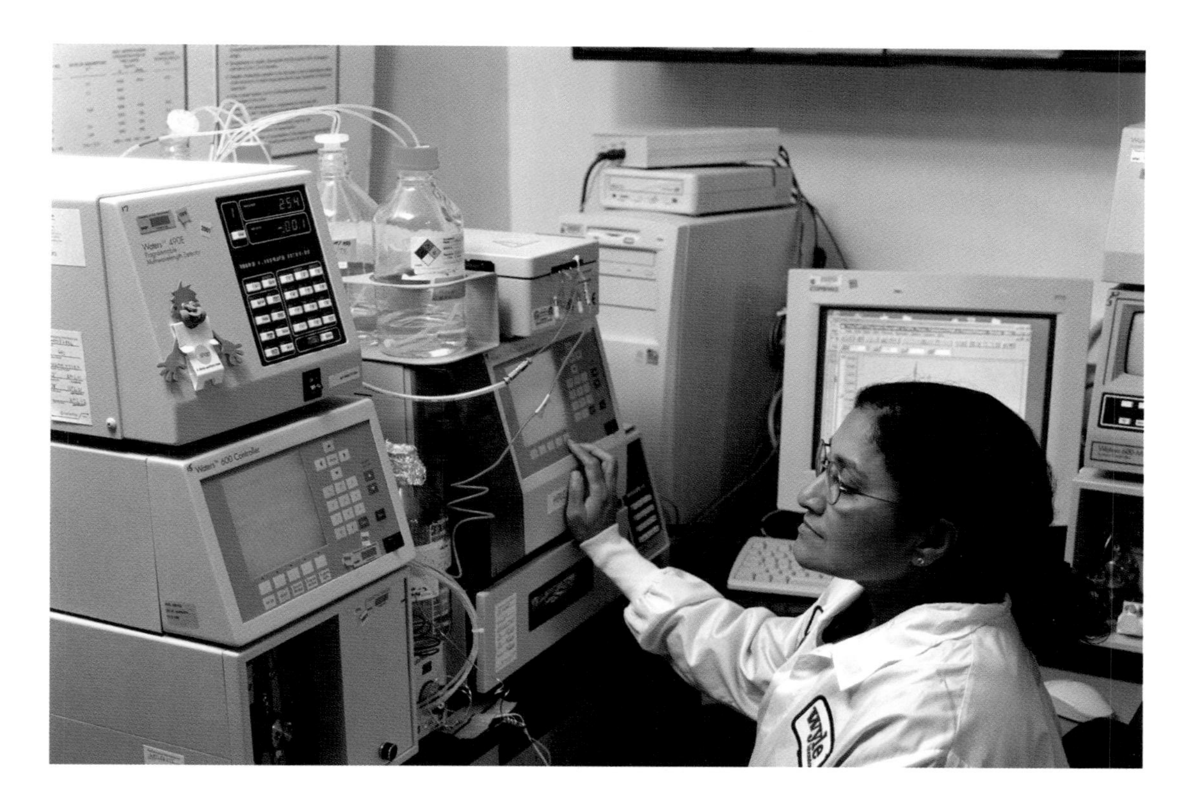

A pharmaceutical technician at work at NASA.

Technologists and Technicians

Technologists and technicians work closely with the engineers and scientists to build, test, and perfect various types of space technology. There are numerous space career opportunities for skilled technologists and technicians in the following fields:

- communications technicians
- computer-aided design (CAD) operators
- **drafters**
- electricians
- laser technicians
- quality assurance specialists
- radar technicians
- robotic technicians
- satellite technologists

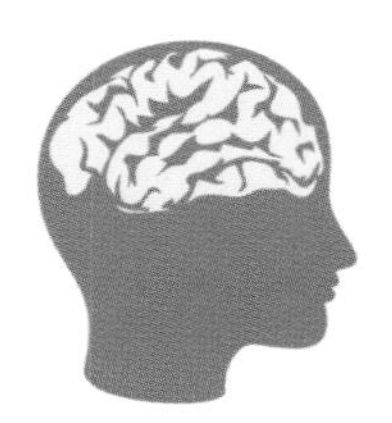

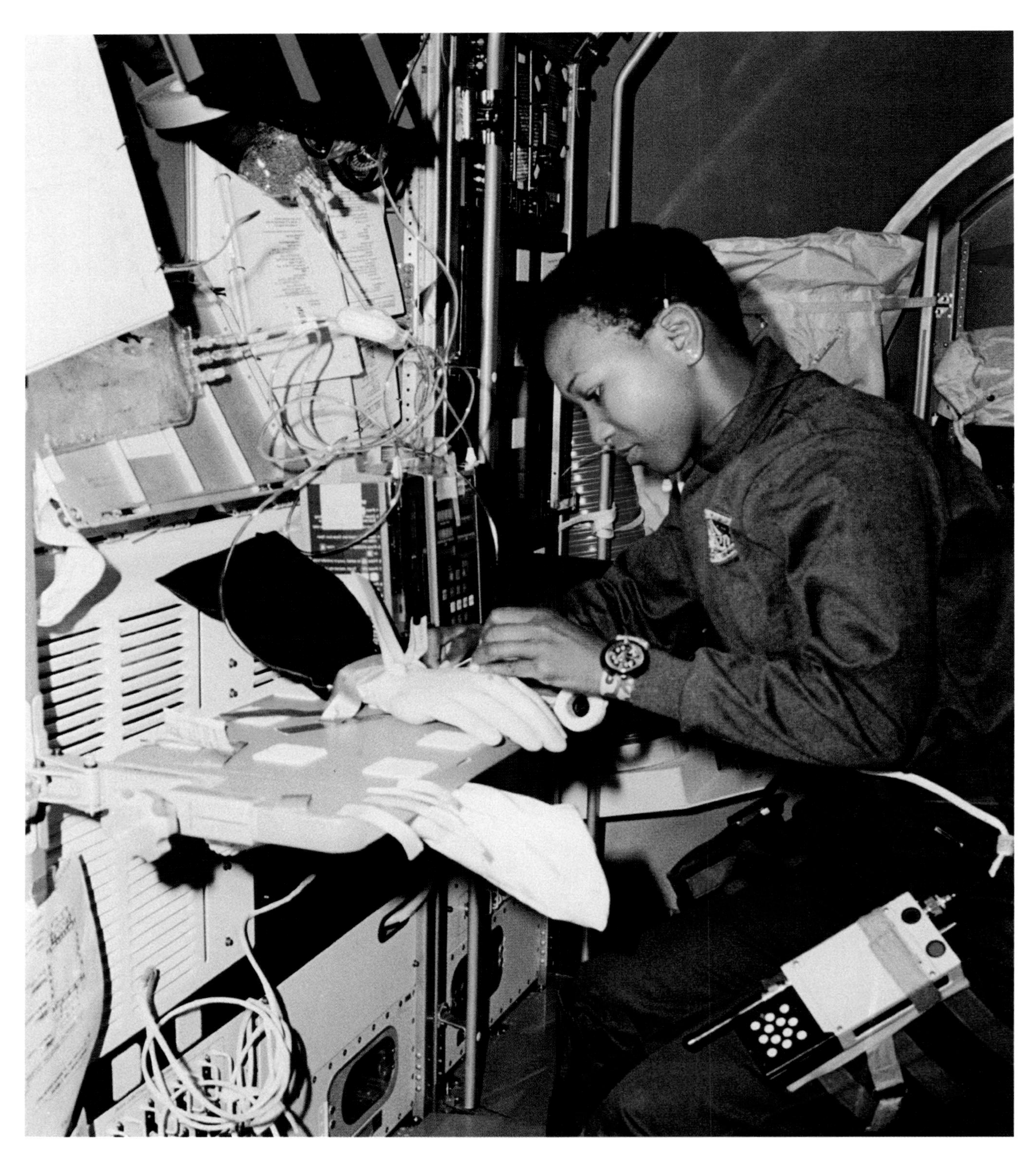

There are all sorts of opportunties for women in space. Here, astronaut Mae Jemison is working on an experiment onboard the space lab. She is injecting fluid into a mannequin's hand as part of a fluid therapy experiment.

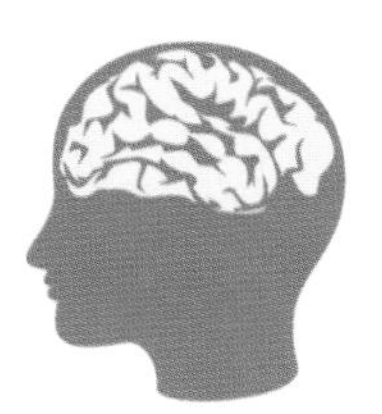

Pursuing a Career in Space Science

Employers who hire space science workers are looking for highly skilled applicants with very specialized training and skills. If you dream of working in this field, you'll need to do your research and work hard. And then—the sky's the limit!

Words to Know

Malfunctions: fails to work right.
Avionics: the application of electronics to planes and space flight.
Research-and-development: activity intended to create or improve products, processes, or knowledge.
Pharmacology: the branch of medicine that focuses on how drugs work, and the best way they can be used.
Geologists: scientists who study the earth's processes and structure.
Meteorologists: scientists who study weather, and who predict weather patterns for the future.
Drafters: people who create technical plans to build products, machines, and buildings.

Find Out More

LovetoKnow Jobs & Careers, "Careers in Space Science"
jobs.lovetoknow.com/Careers_in_Space_Science

Helium, "An Overview on the Types of Jobs Astronauts Perform in Space"
www.helium.com/items/1422222-an-overview-on-the-types-of-jobs-astronauts-perform-in-space

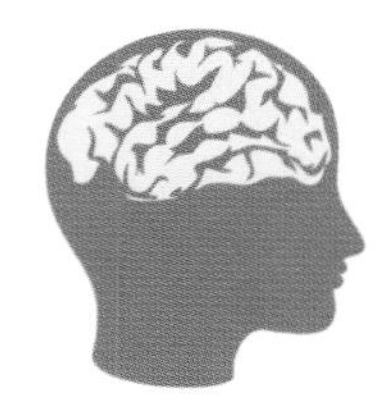

National Aeronautics and Space Administration, “Women @ NASA”
women.nasa.gov

National Aeronautics and Space Administration, “Women in Space.”
history.nasa.gov/women.html

Women in Aerospace: Expanding Women’s Opportunities
www.womeninaerospace.org

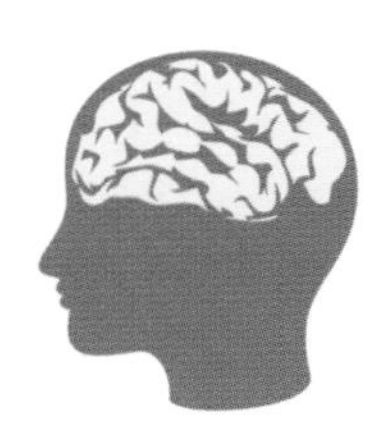

Index

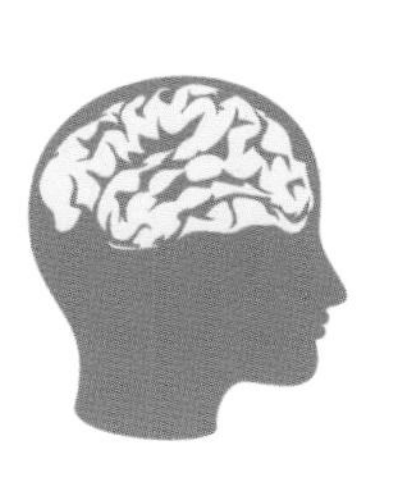

About the Author & Consultant

Shaina Indovino is a writer and illustrator living in Nesconset, New York. She graduated from Binghamton University, where she received degrees in sociology and English. She enjoyed the opportunity to apply both her areas of study to a topic that excites her: women in science. She hopes more young women will follow their calling toward what they truly love, whether it be science related or not.

Ann Lee-Karlon, PhD, is the President of the Association for Women in Science (AWIS) in 2014–2016. AWIS is a national non-profit organization dedicated to advancing women in science, technology, engineering, and mathematics. Dr. Lee-Karlon also serves as Senior Vice President at Genentech, a major biotechnology company focused on discovering and developing medicines for serious diseases such as cancer. Dr. Lee-Karlon holds a BS in Bioengineering from the University of California at Berkeley, an MBA from Stanford University, and a PhD in Bioengineering from the University of California at San Diego, where she was a National Science Foundation Graduate Research Fellow. She completed a postdoctoral fellowship at the University College London as an NSF International Research Fellow. Dr. Lee-Karlon holds several U.S. and international patents in vascular and tissue engineering.

Picture Credits

Alan Poulson (Dreamstime): p. 10
Alexander Mokletstove/RIA Novosti Archives: p. 14
NASA: pp. 8, 17, 24, 28, 32, 36, 38, 40, 46, 48, 52, 54, 55, 56, 59, 60
U.S. National Archives & Records Administration: p. 20

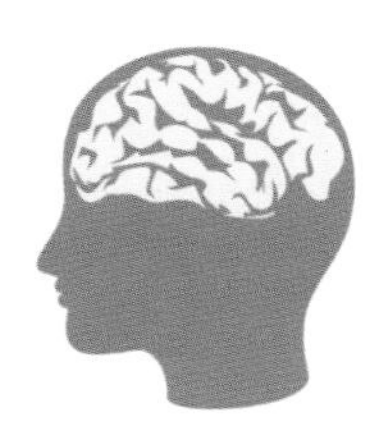